MW01625186

Practical
Chinese

p³

This is a P³ Publishing Book
This edition published in 2004

P³ Publishing
Queen Street House
4 Queen Street
Bath BA1 1HE, UK

ISBN: 1-40543-274-8

Printed in China

NOTE

Cup measurements in this book are for American cups.
This book also uses imperial and metric measurements. Follow the same units of measurement throughout; do not mix imperial and metric.
All spoon measurements are level: teaspoons are assumed to be 5 ml, and tablespoons are assumed to be 15 ml. Unless otherwise stated, milk is assumed to be whole milk, eggs and individual vegetables such as potatoes are medium, and pepper is freshly ground black pepper.

The nutritional information provided for each recipe is per serving or per person. Optional ingredients, variations, or serving suggestions have not been included in the calculations. The times given for each recipe are an approximate guide only because the preparation times may differ according to the techniques used by different people and the cooking times may vary as a result of the type of oven used.

Recipes using raw or very lightly cooked eggs should be avoided by infants, the elderly, pregnant women, convalescents, and anyone suffering from an illness.

Contents

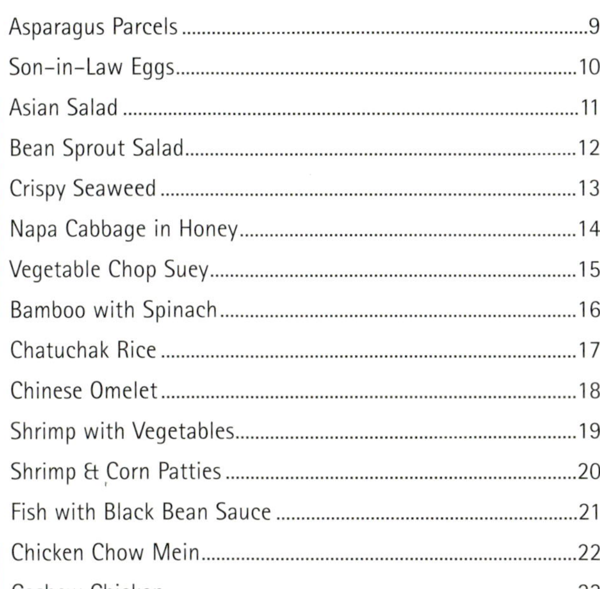

Introduction

The abundance of Chinese restaurants in the West demonstrates perfectly the popularity of Chinese cooking. Authentic dishes from all over China are assembled here for you to try at home. These recipes are delicious, incredibly easy to prepare, and fortunately, for those with a busy lifestyle, many can be cooked in under an hour.

The arrival of Chinese cuisine

Chinese cuisine was introduced to the West when Chinese migrants settled in San Francisco during the Gold Rush. Since then, Chinese restaurants have spread throughout the world and Chinese ingredients and cooking equipment are now readily available.

Benefits of eating Chinese food

Chinese food is generally cooked rapidly over very high heat, using a minimum of oil, which preserves texture, flavor, and nutrients. The ingredients include fish, vegetables, and meats combined with noodles or rice, which are excellent sources of slow, energy-releasing carbohydrates. High-cholesterol ingredients, such as dairy products and red meats, are used sparingly, if at all. Chinese meals are well-balanced, not only in terms of a healthy diet, but also in their aim to provide complementary courses: spicy dishes are served with sweet-and-sour alternatives, dry-cooked dishes are accompanied by those in sauces.

Regional cuisine

China is a vast country with an enormous variety of different climates, which affect the agricultural productivity within each area. The harsh climate around the capital of Beijing in the north is very different to the mild coastal areas of the south; the influence of the Yangtze river is felt strongly at its delta near Shanghai in the east, while the west enjoys a mild, humid climate and rich fertile soil in the shadow of the Tien Shan mountains. The regional cuisines are equally diverse.

The north: dishes from the north are strongly flavored, using leeks, onions, and garlic. Many dishes containing lamb, not pork, bearing testimony to the Moslem culture introduced by invading Tartars from Central Asia. In northern areas, wheat is used more frequently than rice, served as pancakes, noodles, or dumplings.

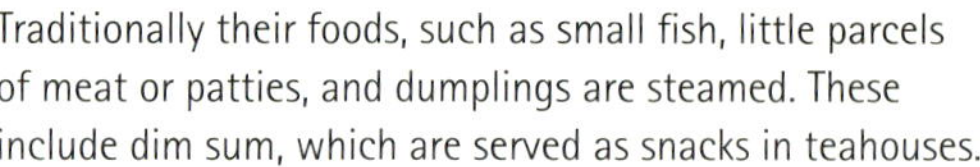

The south: the first emigrant Chinese originated from Canton and its surrounding areas; this is still the most commonly known Chinese regional food in the West. Traditionally their foods, such as small fish, little parcels of meat or patties, and dumplings are steamed. These include dim sum, which are served as snacks in teahouses.

The east: benefiting enormously from the annual flooding of the Yangtze River, the east boasts very rich soil. The fertile plains allow growth of broccoli, sweet potatoes, bok choy, soy beans, tea, and rice—the list is almost endless. Many of the traditional dishes are vegetarian and they vary enormously. Today, the regional cuisines of the east have been influenced by the city of Shanghai, which has assimilated culinary influences from around the world. Dairy products have infiltrated Chinese kitchens, but duck, ham, and fish in piquant spices still remain specialties.

The west: benefiting from a mild climate, Szechuan is noted for its robust, richly colored, spicy dishes. Szechuan cooking uses lots of garlic, ginger, onions, leeks, and Szechuan peppercorns. Western China is renowned for its curing, drying, pickling, and salting techniques, which are used to preserve foods and enhance flavors. Seven different ingredients are used to achieve seven very

particular flavors in Szechuan cooking: sweet flavors use honey; salty ones, soy sauce; sour flavors, vinegar; bitter ones, onions or leeks; fragrant dishes, garlic or ginger; sesame flavors, sesame seed paste; and hot recipes use chiles.

Ingredients

Chinese ingredients are widely available in supermarkets, but it is worth investing in better-quality versions of some of the oils, condiments, and sauces from specialty stores.

Bamboo shoots: fresh bamboo shoots are bland on their own but are used for their texture. Remove tough outer skins, then boil in water for 40–50 minutes.

Bean sauce: available in cans or jars, this savory paste is black or yellow and made from crushed, salted soy beans, flour, and four spices. Red paste is used for sweet sauces.

Chiles: fiery-hot chili oil contains chili flakes and should be used with caution. Chili bean sauce contains soy beans and uses the chilies for flavor—it should also be used sparingly. If using fresh chiles, remember that small, pointed chiles are usually much hotter than larger, more rounded ones. Parts containing seeds are the hottest, so removing these will reduce the potency of the chiles.

Chinese five-spice: the five spices are fennel seeds, cinnamon, cloves, star anise, and Szechuan pepper. They produce a musty, pungent aroma and add a delicious and distinctive flavor.

Chinese rice wine and vinegar: rice wine is made from glutinous rice and resembles dry sherry (which can be used as a suitable alternative in Chinese cooking). Rice vinegar is distilled from Chinese rice wine and is stronger than red vinegar. Cider vinegar or white wine vinegar can be used instead.

Dried mushrooms: shiitake mushrooms have a strong flavor; they are expensive but a little goes a long way. The dried mushrooms need to be soaked for 20–30 minutes before use; the water can be kept for bouillon.

Ginger: gingerroot can be bought in the supermarket: look for plump pieces with shiny, unblemished skin. Cut the amount you need, peel it, then chop, slice, or grate it. Fresh ginger will keep for weeks in a cool, dry place. Ground ginger is not a good substitute.

Lemongrass: the lower part of lemongrass stems add a slightly citrus flavor to a dish. If used whole, lemongrass should be removed before serving.

Peking sauce: made from soy beans, sugar, flour, vinegar, chiles, garlic, sesame oil, and salt. It is used for flavoring in small quantities combined with soy sauce or used alone on duck, spare ribs, or seafood.

Star anise: this is a star-shaped fruit with a strong anise flavor. It is usually used ground. Pods can also be used but they should be removed before serving.

Cooking equipment

A good-quality wok is essential if you want to achieve an authentic Chinese taste. Traditionally made from cast iron, there are now many different types of wok. Stainless steel woks are not recommended, however, because they scorch, and some nonstick woks cannot tolerate the very high temperatures required. To cook food evenly, it should be tossed or stirred continuously. There are few special accessories required for Chinese cooking. A lid for your wok is essential for steaming. Cleavers are used to chop, dice, and cut everything from shellfish and herbs, to meat and vegetables. Chopsticks are used for preparation—they are unlikely to damage delicate food—as well as for eating.

KEY

 Simplicity level 1–3 (1 easiest, 3 slightly harder)

 Preparation time

 Cooking time

Mushroom Noodle Soup

A light, refreshing, clear soup of mushrooms, cucumber, and small pieces of rice noodles, flavored with soy sauce and a touch of garlic.

NUTRITIONAL INFORMATION

Calories	84	Sugars	1g
Protein	1g	Fat	8g
Carbohydrate	3g	Saturates	1g

 5 mins  10 mins

SERVES 4

INGREDIENTS

- 4½ oz/125 g flat or open-cup mushrooms
- ½ cucumber
- 2 scallions
- 1 garlic clove
- 2 tbsp vegetable oil
- ¼ cup Chinese rice noodles
- ¾ tsp salt
- 1 tbsp soy sauce

1 Wash the mushrooms and pat dry on paper towels. Slice thinly. Do not peel them because this adds more flavor.

2 Halve the cucumber lengthwise. Using a teaspoon, scoop out the seeds, and slice the cucumber thinly.

3 Finely chop the scallions and cut the garlic clove into thin strips.

4 Heat the vegetable oil in a large pan or wok.

5 Add the chopped scallions and garlic strips to the pan or wok and then stir-fry them for 30 seconds. Add the thinly sliced mushrooms and stir-fry for 2–3 minutes.

6 Stir in 2½ cups water. Break the noodles into short lengths and add them to the soup. Bring the soup to a boil, stirring occasionally.

7 Add the cucumber slices, salt, and soy sauce, and simmer for 2–3 minutes.

8 Serve the mushroom noodle soup in warmed bowls, distributing the noodles and vegetables evenly.

COOK'S TIP

Scooping out the seeds from the cucumber gives it a prettier effect when sliced, and also helps to reduce any bitterness, but if you prefer, you can leave them in.

Chicken & Corn Soup

This warming, creamy chicken soup is made into a meal in itself with the addition of strands of vermicelli.

NUTRITIONAL INFORMATION			
Calories	401	Sugars	6g
Protein	31g	Fat	24g
Carbohydrate	17g	Saturates	13g

 5 mins — 25 mins

SERVES 4

INGREDIENTS

- 1 lb/450 g boned chicken breasts, cut into strips
- 5 cups chicken bouillon
- ⅔ cup heavy cream
- 3½ oz/100 g dried vermicelli
- 1 tbsp cornstarch
- 3 tbsp milk
- 6 oz/175 g corn kernels
- salt and pepper

1

4

4

1 Put the chicken strips, bouillon, and heavy cream into a large pan and bring to a boil over low heat. Lower the heat slightly and then simmer for about 20 minutes. Season the soup with salt and pepper to taste.

2 Meanwhile, cook the vermicelli in lightly salted boiling water for 10–12 minutes, or until just tender. Drain the pasta and keep warm.

3 In a small bowl, mix together the cornstarch and milk to make a smooth paste. Stir the cornstarch mixture into the soup, until it has thickened.

4 Add the corn kernels and vermicelli to the pan and heat through.

5 Transfer the soup to a warm serving bowl or individual soup bowls and serve immediately.

COOK'S TIP

If you are short of time, buy ready-cooked chicken, remove any skin, and cut it into slices.

Chinese Potato & Pork Broth

In this recipe the pork is seasoned with traditional Chinese flavorings—soy sauce, rice wine vinegar, and a dash of sesame oil.

NUTRITIONAL INFORMATION

Calories	166	Sugars	2g
Protein	10g	Fat	5g
Carbohydrate	26g	Saturates	1g

 5 mins  20 mins

SERVES 4

INGREDIENTS

- 4½ cups chicken bouillon
- 3½ cups diced potatoes
- 2 tbsp rice wine vinegar
- 2 tbsp cornstarch
- 4 tbsp water
- 4½ oz/125 g pork fillet, sliced
- 1 tbsp light soy sauce
- 1 tsp sesame oil
- 1 carrot, cut into thin strips
- 1 tsp chopped fresh gingerroot
- 3 scallions, thinly sliced
- 1 red bell pepper, sliced
- 8 oz/225 g canned bamboo shoots, drained

4

5

5

1 Add the chicken bouillon, diced potatoes, and 1 tablespoon of the rice wine vinegar to a pan and bring to a boil. Lower the heat until just simmering.

2 Mix the cornstarch with the water, then stir into the hot bouillon.

3 Bring the bouillon back to a boil, stirring until thickened, then lower the heat until it is just simmering again.

4 Put the pork slices in a dish and mix with the remaining rice wine vinegar, the soy sauce, and the sesame oil.

5 Add the pork slices and their liquid to the bouillon along with the carrot and ginger. Cook for 10 minutes. Stir in the scallions, red bell pepper, and bamboo shoots. Cook for another 5 minutes. Pour the soup into warmed bowls and then serve immediately.

VARIATION

For extra heat, add 1 chopped red chile or 1 teaspoon of chili powder to the soup in step 5.

Asparagus Parcels

These small parcels are ideal as part of a main meal and irresistible as a quick snack with extra plum sauce for dipping.

NUTRITIONAL INFORMATION	
Calories 194	Sugars 2g
Protein 3g	Fat 16g
Carbohydrate 11g	Saturates 4g

 5 mins  25 mins

SERVES 4

INGREDIENTS

- 3½ oz/100 g fine-tipped asparagus
- 1 red bell pepper, seeded and thinly sliced
- ½ cup bean sprouts
- 2 tbsp plum sauce
- 1 egg yolk
- 8 sheets phyllo pastry
- oil, for deep-frying

2

5

6

1 Place the asparagus, bell pepper, and bean sprouts in a large mixing bowl.

2 Add the plum sauce to the vegetables and mix until well combined.

3 Beat the egg yolk and set aside until required.

4 Lay the sheets of phyllo pastry out on a clean counter.

5 Place a little of the asparagus and red bell pepper filling at the top end of each phyllo pastry sheet. Brush the edges of the phyllo pastry with a little of the beaten egg yolk.

6 Roll up the phyllo pastry, tucking in the ends, and enclosing the filling like a spring roll. Repeat with the remaining phyllo sheets.

7 Heat the oil for deep-frying in a large preheated wok. Carefully cook the parcels, 2 at a time, in the hot oil for 4–5 minutes, or until crispy.

8 Remove the cooked parcels with a slotted spoon and let them drain on paper towels.

9 Transfer the parcels to warm serving plates and serve immediately.

COOK'S TIP

Be sure to use fine-tipped asparagus because it is more tender than the larger stems.

Son-in-Law Eggs

This recipe is supposedly so called because it is an easy dish for a son-in-law to cook to impress his new mother-in-law!

NUTRITIONAL INFORMATION

Calories	229	Sugars	8g
Protein	9g	Fat	18g
Carbohydrate	8g	Saturates	3g

 15 mins  15 mins

SERVES 4

INGREDIENTS

- 6 hard-cooked eggs
- 4 tbsp sunflower oil
- 1 onion, thinly sliced
- 2 fresh red chiles, sliced
- 2 tbsp sugar
- 1 tbsp water
- 2 tsp tamarind pulp
- 1 tbsp liquid seasoning, such as Maggi
- freshly cooked rice, to serve

1 Shell the hard-cooked eggs and then prick each one 2 or 3 times with a toothpick.

2 Heat the sunflower oil in a wok and add the eggs. Cook them in the wok until crispy and golden. Drain the eggs on absorbent paper towels.

3 Halve the eggs lengthwise and put them on a serving dish.

4 Reserve one tablespoon of the oil, drain off the rest, then heat the reserved tablespoonful in the wok. Cook the sliced onion and chiles over high heat, until golden and slightly crisp. Drain on paper towels.

5 Heat the sugar, water, tamarind pulp, and liquid seasoning in the wok and simmer for 5 minutes, until thickened.

6 Pour the sauce over the eggs and spoon over the onion and chiles. Serve immediately with cooked rice.

COOK'S TIP

Tamarind pulp is sold in Asian stores, and is quite sour. If it is not available, use twice the amount of lemon juice in its place.

Asian Salad

This colorful, crisp salad has a fresh orange dressing and is topped with crunchy vermicelli.

NUTRITIONAL INFORMATION

Calories	139	Sugars	8g
Protein	5g	Fat	7g
Carbohydrate	15g	Saturates	1g

10 mins   5 mins

SERVES 4

INGREDIENTS

¼ cup dried vermicelli

½ head napa cabbage

2 cups bean sprouts

6 radishes

4½ oz/125 g snow peas

1 large carrot

4½ oz/125 g sprouting beans

DRESSING

juice of 1 orange

1 tbsp sesame seeds, toasted

1 tsp honey

1 tsp sesame oil

1 tbsp hazelnut oil

1 Break the vermicelli into small strands. Heat a wok and cook the vermicelli in the dry pan until lightly golden.

2 Remove from the pan with a slotted spoon and set aside until required.

3 Using a sharp knife or food processor, shred the napa cabbage and wash with the bean sprouts. Drain thoroughly and place the leaves and bean sprouts in a large mixing bowl.

4 Thinly slice the radishes. Trim the snow peas and cut each into 3 pieces. Cut the carrot into thin matchsticks. Add the sprouting beans and prepared vegetables to the bowl.

5 Place all the dressing ingredients in a screw-top jar and shake well. Pour over the salad and toss together.

6 Transfer the salad to a serving bowl and sprinkle over the crispy vermicelli before serving.

COOK'S TIP

Make your own sprouting beans by soaking mung and adzuki beans overnight in cold water; drain and rinse. Place in a large jar covered with cheesecloth to secure it. Lay the jar on its side and place in indirect light. For the next 3 days, rinse the beans once each day in cold water, until ready to eat.

Bean Sprout Salad

This is a very light dish and is ideal on its own for a summer meal or as an appetizer.

NUTRITIONAL INFORMATION

Calories	70	Sugars	5g
Protein	4g	Fat	3g
Carbohydrate	7g	Saturates	0.5g

 10 mins  5 mins

SERVES 4

INGREDIENTS

- 1 green bell pepper, seeded
- 1 carrot
- 1 celery stick
- 2 tomatoes
- 12 oz/350 g bean sprouts
- 1 small cucumber
- 1 garlic clove, crushed
- dash of chili sauce
- 2 tbsp light soy sauce
- 1 tsp wine vinegar
- 2 tsp sesame oil
- 16 fresh chives

1 Using a sharp knife, cut the green bell pepper, carrot, and celery into matchsticks and then finely chop the tomatoes.

2 Blanch the bean sprouts in boiling water for 1 minute. Drain well and rinse under cold water. Drain them again thoroughly.

3 Cut the cucumber in half lengthwise. Scoop out the seeds with a teaspoon and discard them. Cut the flesh into matchsticks.

4 Mix the cucumber with the bean sprouts, green bell pepper, carrot, tomatoes, and celery.

5 To make the dressing, mix together the garlic, chili sauce, soy sauce, wine vinegar, and sesame oil in a small bowl.

6 Pour the dressing over the vegetables, tossing together until well coated.

7 Spoon the bean sprout salad into a serving dish or onto 4 individual serving plates. Garnish the salad with fresh chives and serve.

2

4

6

VARIATION

Substitute 12 oz/350 g cooked, cooled green beans or snow peas for the cucumber. Vary the bean sprouts for a different flavor. Try adzuki bean or alfalfa sprouts, as well as the better-known mung and soy bean sprouts.

Crispy Seaweed

This tasty Chinese appetizer is not all that it seems—the "seaweed" is in fact bok choy, which is then cooked, salted, and tossed with pine nuts.

NUTRITIONAL INFORMATION	
Calories 214	Sugars 14g
Protein 6g	Fat 15g
Carbohydrate . . .15g	Saturates 2g

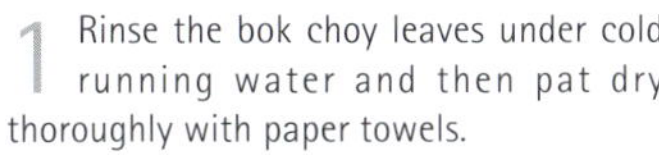

SERVES 4

INGREDIENTS

- 2 lb 4 oz/1 kg bok choy
- 3½ cups peanut oil, for deep-frying
- 1 tsp salt
- 1 tbsp superfine sugar
- 2½ tbsp pine nuts, toasted

1 Rinse the bok choy leaves under cold running water and then pat dry thoroughly with paper towels.

2 Discarding any tough outer leaves, roll up each bok choy leaf, then slice through thinly so that the leaves are finely shredded. Alternatively, use a food processor to shred the bok choy.

3 Heat the peanut oil in a large wok or heavy-bottomed skillet.

4 Carefully add the shredded bok choy leaves to the wok or skillet and cook for about 30 seconds, or until they shrivel up and become crispy (you will probably need to do this in several batches, depending on the size of your wok).

5 Use a strainer or slotted spoon to lift out the crispy seaweed from the wok and drain on paper towels.

6 Transfer the crispy seaweed to a large bowl and toss with the salt, sugar, and pine nuts. Serve immediately on warm serving plates.

COOK'S TIP

The tough, outer leaves of bok choy are discarded because these will spoil the overall taste and texture of the dish. If bok choy is unavailable, use savoy cabbage instead, drying the leaves thoroughly before cooking.

Napa Cabbage in Honey

Napa cabbage is somewhat similar to lettuce in that the leaves are delicate with a sweet flavor.

NUTRITIONAL INFORMATION

Calories	121	Sugars	6g
Protein	5g	Fat	7g
Carbohydrate	10g	Saturates	1g

 5 mins  10 mins

SERVES 4

INGREDIENTS

1 lb/450 g napa cabbage

1 tbsp peanut oil

1 tsp grated fresh gingerroot

2 garlic cloves, crushed

1 fresh red chile, sliced

1 tbsp Chinese rice wine or dry sherry

4½ tsp light soy sauce

1 tbsp clear honey

½ cup orange juice

1 tbsp sesame oil

2 tsp sesame seeds

strips of orange zest, to garnish

1

3

4

1 Separate the napa cabbage and shred the leaves finely, using a sharp knife.

2 Heat the peanut oil in a preheated wok. Add the ginger, garlic, and chile to the wok and cook the mixture for about 30 seconds.

3 Add the napa cabbage, Chinese rice wine or sherry, soy sauce, honey, and orange juice to the wok. Lower the heat and let simmer for 5 minutes.

4 Add the sesame oil to the wok, sprinkle the sesame seeds over the top, and mix to combine.

5 Transfer to a warm serving dish, garnish with the orange zest, and serve immediately.

COOK'S TIP

Single-flower honey has a better, more individual flavor than blended honey. Acacia honey is typically Chinese, but you could also try clover, lemon blossom, lime flower, or orange blossom honey.

Vegetable Chop Suey

Make sure that the vegetables are all cut into pieces of a similar size in this recipe, so that they cook within the same amount of time.

NUTRITIONAL INFORMATION			
Calories	155	Sugars	6g
Protein	4g	Fat	12g
Carbohydrate	9g	Saturates	2g

 5 mins  5 mins

SERVES 4

INGREDIENTS

- 1 yellow bell pepper, seeded
- 1 red bell pepper, seeded
- 1 carrot
- 1 zucchini
- 1 fennel bulb
- 1 onion
- 2 oz/60 g snow peas
- 2 tbsp peanut oil
- 3 garlic cloves, crushed
- 1 tsp grated fresh gingerroot
- 1¼ cups bean sprouts
- 2 tsp light brown sugar
- 2 tbsp light soy sauce
- ½ cup vegetable bouillon

1

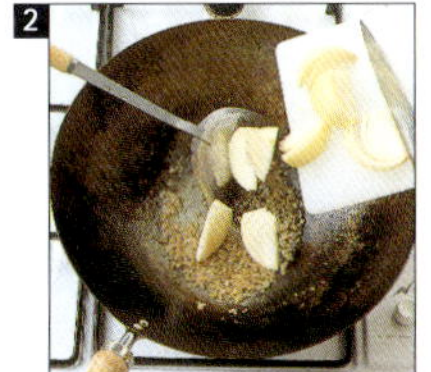

2

3

1 Cut the bell peppers, carrot, zucchini, and fennel into thin slices. Cut the onion into fourths, then cut each fourth in half. Slice the snow peas diagonally to create the maximum surface area.

2 Heat the oil in a preheated wok, add the garlic and ginger and cook for 30 seconds. Add the onion and cook for another 30 seconds.

3 Add the bell peppers, carrot, zucchini, fennel, and snow peas to the wok and cook for 2 minutes.

4 Add the bean sprouts to the wok and stir in the sugar, soy sauce, and bouillon. Reduce the heat to low and simmer for about 1–2 minutes, until the vegetables are tender and coated in the sauce.

5 Transfer the vegetables and sauce to a serving dish and serve immediately.

VARIATION

Use any combination of colorful vegetables that you have at hand to make this versatile dish.

Bamboo with Spinach

In this recipe, spinach is cooked with spices and then braised in a soy-flavored sauce with bamboo shoots for a rich, delicious dish.

NUTRITIONAL INFORMATION

Calories	105	Sugars	1g
Protein	3g	Fat	9g
Carbohydrate	3g	Saturates	2g

 5 mins 10 mins

SERVES 4

INGREDIENTS

- 3 tbsp peanut oil
- 8 oz/225 g spinach, chopped
- 6 oz/175 g canned bamboo shoots, drained and rinsed
- 1 garlic clove, crushed
- 2 fresh red chiles, sliced
- pinch of ground cinnamon
- 1¼ cups vegetable bouillon
- pinch of sugar
- pinch of salt
- 1 tbsp light soy sauce
- 1 tsp cornstarch (optional)

2

3

4

1 Heat the peanut oil in a preheated wok or large skillet, swirling the oil around the bottom of the wok until it is really hot.

2 Add the spinach and bamboo shoots to the wok and cook for 1 minute.

3 Add the garlic, chiles, and cinnamon to the mixture in the wok and cook for another 30 seconds.

4 Stir in the bouillon, sugar, salt, and light soy sauce, cover, and cook over medium heat for 5 minutes, or until the vegetables are cooked through and the sauce has reduced. If there is too much cooking liquid, blend 1 teaspoon of cornstarch with 2 teaspoons of cold water and stir into the sauce.

5 Transfer the bamboo shoots and spinach to a serving dish and serve.

COOK'S TIP

Fresh bamboo shoots are rarely available in the West and, in any case, are extremely time-consuming to prepare. Canned bamboo shoots are quite satisfactory, because they are used for their crunchy texture, not their flavor, which is fairly insipid.

Chatuchak Rice

An excellent way to use up leftover rice. Pop it in the freezer as soon as it is cool, and it will be ready to reheat at any time.

NUTRITIONAL INFORMATION			
Calories	241	Sugars	5g
Protein	7g	Fat	5g
Carbohydrate	46g	Saturates	1g

 25 mins  15 mins

SERVES 4

INGREDIENTS

- 1 tbsp sunflower oil
- 3 shallots, finely chopped
- 2 garlic cloves, crushed
- 1 red chile, seeded and finely chopped
- 1-inch/2.5-cm piece gingerroot, finely shredded
- ½ green bell pepper, seeded and finely sliced
- 5½ oz/150 g baby eggplants, cut into fourths
- 3 oz/90 g sugar snap peas or snow peas, trimmed and blanched
- 3 oz/90 g baby corn, halved lengthwise and blanched
- 1 tomato, cut into 8 pieces
- 1½ cups bean sprouts
- 3 cups cooked jasmine rice
- 2 tbsp tomato catsup
- 2 tbsp light soy sauce

TO GARNISH

- fresh cilantro leaves
- lime wedges

1. Heat the sunflower oil in a wok or large, heavy skillet over high heat.

2. Add the shallots, garlic, chile, and ginger to the wok or skillet. Stir until the shallots have softened.

3. Add the green bell pepper and baby eggplants to the pan and stir well.

4. Add the sugar snap peas or snow peas, baby corn, tomato, and bean sprouts. Stir-fry for 3 minutes.

5. Add the cooked jasmine rice to the wok, and lift and stir with two spoons for 4–5 minutes, until no more steam is released.

6. Stir the tomato catsup and soy sauce into the mixture in the wok.

7. Serve the rice immediately, garnished with sprigs of fresh cilantro, and lime wedges for squeezing over the rice.

Chinese Omelet

This omelet contains chicken and shrimp. It is cooked as a whole omelet and then sliced for serving as part of a Chinese meal.

NUTRITIONAL INFORMATION

Calories	309	Sugars	0g
Protein	34g	Fat	19g
Carbohydrate	0.2g	Saturates	5g

 5 mins  5 mins

SERVES 4

INGREDIENTS

- 8 eggs
- 8 oz/225 g cooked chicken, shredded
- 12 jumbo shrimp, peeled and deveined
- 2 tbsp chopped fresh chives
- 2 tsp light soy sauce
- dash of chili sauce
- 2 tbsp vegetable oil

1

3

4

1 Lightly beat the eggs in a large mixing bowl. Add the shredded chicken and jumbo shrimp and mix well.

2 Stir in the chopped chives, light soy sauce, and chili sauce, mixing well to combine all the ingredients.

3 Heat the vegetable oil in a large, heavy-bottomed skillet over medium heat. Pour in the egg mixture, tilting the pan to coat the bottom evenly and completely. Cook the eggs over medium heat, gently stirring the omelet with a fork to let the raw egg run underneath the set egg, until the surface is just set and the underside is a golden brown color.

4 When the omelet is set, slide it out of the pan with the aid of a spatula. Cut the Chinese omelet into squares or slices and serve immediately.

VARIATION

You could add extra flavor to the omelet by stirring in 3 tablespoons of finely chopped fresh cilantro or 1 teaspoon of sesame seeds with the chives in step 2.

Shrimp with Vegetables

This colorful and delicious dish is cooked with vegetables: vary them according to seasonal availability.

NUTRITIONAL INFORMATION	
Calories 298	Sugars 1g
Protein 13g	Fat 26g
Carbohydrate 3g	Saturates 3g

 5 mins  10 mins

SERVES 4

INGREDIENTS

- 2 oz/60 g snow peas
- ½ small carrot
- 2 oz/60 g baby corn
- 2 oz/60 g straw mushrooms
- 6–9 oz/175–250 g raw jumbo shrimp, peeled
- 1 tsp salt
- ½ egg white, lightly beaten
- 1 tsp cornstarch
- 1¼ cups vegetable oil
- 1 scallion, cut into short sections
- 4 slices gingerroot, peeled and finely chopped
- ½ tsp sugar
- 1 tbsp light soy sauce
- 1 tsp Chinese rice wine or dry sherry
- a few drops of sesame oil

TO GARNISH

- lemon slices
- fresh chives

1 Using a sharp knife, top and tail the snow peas. Cut the carrot into the same size as the snow peas. Halve the baby corn and straw mushrooms.

2 Put the shrimp, a pinch of the salt, and the egg white into a bowl. Mix the cornstarch with 2 teaspoons of water and add to the bowl. Mix together until the shrimp are evenly coated.

3 Preheat a wok over high heat for 2–3 minutes, then add the vegetable oil and heat it to medium-hot.

4 Add the shrimp to the wok, stirring to separate them. Remove the shrimp with a slotted spoon as soon as their color changes.

5 Pour off the oil, leaving about 1 tablespoon in the wok. Add the snow peas, carrot, corn, mushrooms, and scallions. Then add the shrimp, together with the ginger, sugar, soy sauce, and rice wine or sherry, and blend well.

6 Sprinkle over the sesame oil and serve hot, garnished with lemon slices and fresh chives.

Shrimp & Corn Patties

Chopped small shrimp and corn are combined in a light batter, which is dropped in spoonfuls into hot fat to make these tasty patties.

NUTRITIONAL INFORMATION

Calories	250	Sugars	1g
Protein	17g	Fat	9g
Carbohydrate	26g	Saturates	2g

 35 mins  20 mins

SERVES 4

INGREDIENTS

- 1 cup all-purpose flour
- 1½ tsp baking powder
- ½ tsp salt
- 2 eggs
- about 1 cup cold water
- 1 garlic clove, very finely chopped
- 3 scallions, trimmed and very finely chopped
- 1 cup peeled small shrimp, chopped
- ½ cup canned corn, drained
- vegetable oil, for cooking
- pepper

TO GARNISH

- scallion tassels (see Cook's Tip, below)
- chile flowers (see Cook's Tip, below)
- slices of fresh lime

1

1

2

1 Sift the flour, baking powder, and ½ teaspoon salt into a bowl. Add the eggs and half the water and beat to make a smooth batter, adding extra water to give the consistency of heavy cream. Add the garlic and scallions. Cover and set aside for 30 minutes.

2 Stir the small shrimp and the corn into the batter. Season with pepper.

3 Heat 2–3 tablespoons of oil in a wok. Drop tablespoonfuls of the batter into the wok and cook over medium heat, until bubbles rise and the surface just sets. Flip the patties over and cook them on the other side, until golden brown. Drain on paper towels.

4 Cook the remaining batter in the same way, adding more oil to the wok as required. Garnish with the scallion tassels, chile flowers, and slices of fresh lime and serve at once.

COOK'S TIP

To make a scallion tassel or chile flower, hold the stem and make slits almost down its full length several times with a sharp knife. Place in iced water to make it fan out. Remove any chile seeds.

Fish with Black Bean Sauce

Steaming is one of the preferred methods of cooking whole fish in China because it maintains both the flavor and the texture.

NUTRITIONAL INFORMATION

Calories	292	Sugars	3g
Protein	44g	Fat	7g
Carbohydrate	6g	Saturates	0.4g

 10 mins

10 mins

SERVES 4

INGREDIENTS

- 2 lb/900 g whole snapper, cleaned and scaled
- 3 garlic cloves, crushed
- 2 tbsp black bean sauce
- 1 tsp cornstarch
- 2 tsp sesame oil
- 2 tbsp light soy sauce
- 2 tsp superfine sugar
- 2 tbsp dry sherry
- 1 leek, shredded
- 1 small, red bell pepper, seeded and cut into thin strips
- lemon wedges, to garnish
- boiled rice or noodles, to serve

1 Rinse the fish inside and out with cold running water and pat dry with paper towels.

2 Make 2–3 diagonal slashes in the flesh on each side of the fish, using a sharp knife. Rub the garlic into the fish.

3 Combine the black bean sauce, cornstarch, sesame oil, light soy sauce, sugar, and dry sherry in a bowl.

4 Place the fish in a shallow, heatproof dish and pour the sauce mixture over the top. Sprinkle the shredded leek (reserve some for garnish) and bell pepper strips on top of the sauce.

5 Place the dish in the top of a steamer, cover, and steam for 10 minutes, or until the fish is cooked through.

6 Transfer the fish to a serving dish, garnish with shredded leek and lemon wedges, and serve with rice or noodles.

COOK'S TIP

Insert the point of a sharp knife into the fish to test if it is cooked. If the knife goes into the flesh easily, the fish is cooked through.

Chicken Chow Mein

This classic dish requires no introduction because it is already a favorite among many people in the West.

NUTRITIONAL INFORMATION

Calories	230	Sugars	2g
Protein	19g	Fat	11g
Carbohydrate	14g	Saturates	2g

 5 mins 20 mins

SERVES 4

INGREDIENTS

- 9 oz/250 g medium egg noodles
- 2 tbsp sunflower oil
- 9½ oz/275 g cooked chicken breasts, shredded
- 1 garlic clove, finely chopped
- 1 red bell pepper, seeded and thinly sliced
- 3½ oz/100 g shiitake mushrooms, sliced
- 6 scallions, sliced
- 1 cup bean sprouts
- 3 tbsp soy sauce
- 1 tbsp sesame oil

1 Place the egg noodles in a large, heatproof bowl or dish and break them up slightly. Pour over enough boiling water to cover the noodles and let stand.

2 Heat the sunflower oil in a large, preheated wok or skillet. Add the shredded chicken, finely chopped garlic, bell pepper slices, mushrooms, scallions, and bean sprouts to the pan and cook for about 5 minutes.

3 Drain the noodles thoroughly. Add the noodles to the pan, toss well, and cook for another 5 minutes.

4 Drizzle the soy sauce and sesame oil over the chow mein and toss until well combined.

5 Remove the chicken chow mein from the heat, transfer to warm serving bowls, and serve immediately.

1

2

3

VARIATION

You can make the chow mein with a selection of vegetables for a vegetarian dish, if you prefer.

Cashew Chicken

Yellow bean sauce is available from large food stores. Try to buy a chunky sauce instead of a smooth sauce for added texture.

NUTRITIONAL INFORMATION

Calories	398	Sugars	2g
Protein	31g	Fat	27g
Carbohydrate	8g	Saturates	4g

10 mins 15 mins

SERVES 4

INGREDIENTS

- 1 lb/450 g boneless chicken breasts
- 2 tbsp vegetable oil
- 1 red onion, sliced
- 6 oz/175 g flat mushrooms, sliced
- ⅓ cup cashews
- 2¾ oz/75 g yellow bean sauce
- fresh cilantro, chopped, to garnish
- egg fried rice or plain boiled rice, to serve

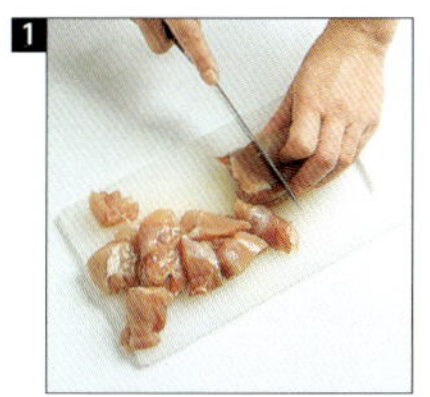

1

3

4

1 Using a sharp knife, remove the excess skin from the chicken breasts, if desired. Cut the chicken into small, bite-size chunks.

2 Heat the vegetable oil in a preheated wok or skillet.

3 Add the chicken to the wok and stir-fry for 5 minutes.

4 Add the red onion and mushrooms to the wok and continue to stir-fry for another 5 minutes.

5 Place the cashews on a cookie sheet and toast under a preheated medium broiler, until just browning—toasting nuts brings out their flavor.

6 Toss the toasted cashews into the wok together with the yellow bean sauce and heat through. Let the sauce bubble for 2–3 minutes.

7 Transfer to warm serving bowls and garnish with chopped fresh cilantro. Serve hot with egg fried rice or plain boiled rice.

VARIATION

Chicken thighs could be used instead of the chicken breasts for a more economical dish.

Duck with Ginger & Lime

Just the thing for a lazy summer day—roasted duck sliced and served with a dressing made from ginger, lime juice, sesame oil, and fish sauce.

NUTRITIONAL INFORMATION

Calories	529	Sugars	3g
Protein	38g	Fat	41g
Carbohydrate	3g	Saturates	6g

20 mins  25 mins

SERVES 4

INGREDIENTS

- 3 boneless Barbary duck breasts, about 9 oz/250 g each
- salt

DRESSING

- ½ cup olive oil
- 2 tsp sesame oil
- 2 tbsp lime juice
- grated zest and juice of 1 orange
- 2 tsp fish sauce
- 1 tbsp grated fresh gingerroot
- 1 garlic clove, crushed
- 2 tsp light soy sauce
- 3 scallions, finely chopped
- 1 tsp sugar
- about 9 oz/250 g assorted salad greens
- orange slices, to garnish (optional)

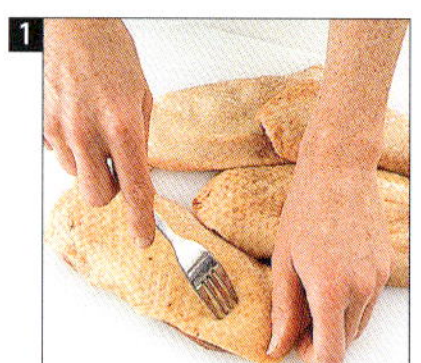

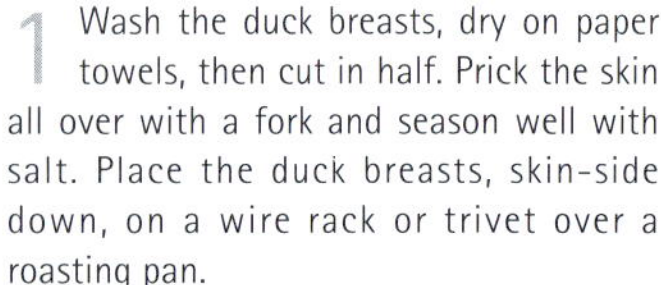

1 Wash the duck breasts, dry on paper towels, then cut in half. Prick the skin all over with a fork and season well with salt. Place the duck breasts, skin-side down, on a wire rack or trivet over a roasting pan.

2 Cook the duck in a preheated oven, 425°F/220°C, for 10 minutes. Turn over and cook for another 12–15 minutes, or until the duck is cooked, but still pink in the center, and the skin is crisp.

3 To make the dressing, beat the olive oil and sesame oil in a nonmetallic bowl, then add the lime juice, orange zest and juice, fish sauce, grated gingerroot, garlic, light soy sauce, scallions, and sugar. Beat together well until the ingredients are thoroughly blended.

4 Remove the duck from the oven, let cool, and cut into thick slices. Add a little dressing to moisten and coat the duck.

5 To serve, arrange the salad greens on a serving dish. Top with the duck and drizzle over the remaining dressing.

6 Garnish with orange slices, if using, then serve at once.

Pork Dim Sum

These small steamed parcels are traditionally served as an appetizer and are very adaptable to your favorite fillings.

NUTRITIONAL INFORMATION	
Calories 478	Sugars 3g
Protein 33g	Fat 29g
Carbohydrate . . .21g	Saturates 9g

 10 mins  15 mins

SERVES 4

INGREDIENTS

- 14 oz/400 g ground pork
- 2 scallions, chopped
- 1¾ oz/50 g canned bamboo shoots, drained, rinsed, and chopped
- 1 tbsp light soy sauce
- 1 tbsp dry sherry
- 2 tsp sesame oil
- 2 tsp superfine sugar
- 1 egg white, lightly beaten
- 4½ tsp cornstarch
- 24 won ton wrappers

2

3

4

1 Place the ground pork, scallions, bamboo shoots, soy sauce, dry sherry, sesame oil, superfine sugar, and beaten egg white in a large mixing bowl and mix together until all the ingredients are thoroughly combined.

2 Stir in the cornstarch, mixing until thoroughly incorporated with the other ingredients.

3 Spread out the won ton wrappers on a clean counter. Place a spoonful of the pork mixture in the center of each wrapper and lightly brush the edges of the wrappers with water. Bring the sides of the wrappers together in the center of the filling, pinching firmly together.

4 Line a steamer with a clean, damp dish cloth and arrange the won tons inside. Cover and steam for 5–7 minutes, until the dim sum are cooked through. Serve immediately.

COOK'S TIP

Bamboo steamers are designed to rest on the sloping sides of a wok above the water. They are available in a range of sizes.

Sweet & Sour Pork

This dish is a popular choice in Western diets, and must be one of the best known of Chinese recipes.

NUTRITIONAL INFORMATION

Calories	471	Sugars	47g
Protein	16g	Fat	13g
Carbohydrate	77g	Saturates	2g

10 mins | 20 mins

SERVES 4

INGREDIENTS

- ⅔ cup vegetable oil, for deep-frying
- 8 oz/225 g pork tenderloin, cut into ½-inch/1-cm cubes
- 1 onion, sliced
- 1 green bell pepper, seeded and sliced
- 8 oz/225 g pineapple pieces
- 1 small carrot, cut into thin strips
- 1 oz/25 g canned bamboo shoots, drained, rinsed, and halved
- cooked rice or noodles, to serve

BATTER

- scant 1 cup all-purpose flour
- 1 tbsp cornstarch
- 1½ tsp baking powder
- 1 tbsp vegetable oil

SAUCE

- ⅔ cup light brown sugar
- 2 tbsp cornstarch
- ½ cup white wine vinegar
- 2 garlic cloves, crushed
- 4 tbsp tomato paste
- 6 tbsp pineapple juice

1 To make the batter, sift the all-purpose flour into a mixing bowl with the cornstarch and baking powder. Add the vegetable oil and stir in enough water to make a thick, smooth batter (about ¾ cup).

2 Pour ⅔ cup of the vegetable oil into a preheated wok and heat until almost smoking.

3 Dip the cubes of pork into the batter, and cook in the hot oil, in batches, until cooked through. Remove the pork from the wok with a slotted spoon and drain on absorbent paper towels. Keep it warm until required.

4 Drain all but 1 tablespoon of oil from the wok and return it to the heat. Add the onion, bell pepper, pineapple pieces, carrot, and bamboo shoots and stir-fry for 1–2 minutes. Remove from the wok with a slotted spoon and set aside.

5 Mix all of the sauce ingredients together and pour into the wok. Bring to a boil, stirring, until thickened and clear. Cook for 1 minute, then return the pork and vegetables to the wok. Cook for another 1–2 minutes, then transfer to a serving plate and serve with rice or noodles.

3

4

5

Pork Chow Mein

This is a basic recipe—the meat and/or vegetables can be varied as much as you like.

NUTRITIONAL INFORMATION

Calories	239	Sugars	1g
Protein	17g	Fat	14g
Carbohydrate	12g	Saturates	2g

 15 mins  15 mins

SERVES 4

INGREDIENTS

- 9 oz/250 g egg noodles
- 4–5 tbsp vegetable oil
- 9 oz/250 g pork tenderloin, cooked
- 4½ oz/125g green beans
- 2 tbsp light soy sauce
- 1 tsp salt
- ½ tsp sugar
- 1 tbsp Chinese rice wine or dry sherry
- 2 scallions, finely shredded
- a few drops of sesame oil
- chili sauce, to serve (optional)

1 Cook the noodles in boiling water according to the instructions on the package, then drain and rinse under cold water. Drain again, then toss with 1 tablespoon of the oil.

2 Slice the pork into thin shreds and top and tail the green beans.

3 Heat 3 tablespoons of oil in a preheated wok until hot. Add the noodles and 1 tablespoon of soy sauce and stir-fry for 2-3 minutes. Remove to a serving dish and keep warm.

4 Heat the remaining oil in the wok, add the green beans and the meat, and stir-fry for 2 minutes. Add the salt, sugar, rice wine or sherry, the remaining soy sauce and about half of the scallions to the wok.

5 Stir the mixture in the wok, adding a little water if necessary, then pour on top of the noodles, and sprinkle with sesame oil and the remaining scallions.

6 Serve the chow mein hot or cold, with chili sauce if using.

COOK'S TIP

"Chow mein" literally means "stir-fried noodles" and is highly popular in the West as well as in China. Almost any ingredient can be added, such as fish, meat, poultry, or vegetables. It is very popular for lunch and makes a tasty salad served cold.

Cantonese Noodles

This dish is usually served as a snack or light meal. It may also be served as an accompaniment to plain meat and fish dishes.

NUTRITIONAL INFORMATION

Calories	385	Sugars	6g
Protein	38g	Fat	17g
Carbohydrate	21g	Saturates	4g

 5 mins  15 mins

SERVES 4

INGREDIENTS

- 12 oz/350 g egg noodles
- 3 tbsp vegetable oil
- 1½ lb/675 g lean beef steak, cut into thin strips
- 4½ oz/125 g green cabbage, shredded
- 2¾ oz/75 g canned bamboo shoots, drained
- 6 scallions, sliced
- 1 oz/25 g green beans, halved
- 1 tbsp dark soy sauce
- 2 tbsp beef bouillon
- 1 tbsp dry sherry
- 1 tbsp light brown sugar
- 2 tbsp chopped fresh parsley, to garnish

1 Cook the noodles in a pan of boiling water for 2–3 minutes. Drain well, rinse under cold running water, and drain thoroughly again.

2 Heat 1 tablespoon of the vegetable oil in a preheated wok or skillet, swirling it around until it is really hot.

3 Add the noodles to the pan and cook for 1–2 minutes. Drain the noodles and set aside until required.

4 Heat the remaining vegetable oil in the wok. Add the beef and cook for 2–3 minutes. Add the cabbage, bamboo shoots, scallions, and green beans to the wok and cook for 1–2 minutes.

5 Add the soy sauce, beef bouillon, dry sherry, and light brown sugar to the wok, and stir to mix.

6 Stir the noodles into the mixture in the wok, tossing to mix well. Transfer to serving bowls, garnish with chopped parsley, and serve immediately.

VARIATION

You can vary the vegetables in this dish depending on seasonal availability or whatever you have at hand—try broccoli, green bell pepper, or spinach.

4

4

5

Soy & Sesame Beef

Soy sauce and sesame seeds are classic ingredients in Chinese cooking. Use a dark soy sauce for fuller flavor and richness.

NUTRITIONAL INFORMATION

Calories	324	Sugars	2g
Protein	25g	Fat	22g
Carbohydrate	3g	Saturates	6g

 5 mins

10 mins

SERVES 4

INGREDIENTS

- 2 tbsp sesame seeds
- 1 lb/450 g beef fillet
- 2 tbsp vegetable oil
- 1 green bell pepper, seeded and thinly sliced
- 4 garlic cloves, crushed
- 2 tbsp dry sherry
- 4 tbsp soy sauce
- 6 scallions, sliced
- freshly boiled noodles, to serve

1 Heat a large wok or heavy-bottomed skillet until it is very hot.

2 Add the sesame seeds to the pan and dry-fry, stirring, for 1–2 minutes, or until they just begin to brown. Remove the sesame seeds from the wok and set aside until required.

3 Using a sharp knife or meat cleaver, thinly slice the beef.

4 Heat the vegetable oil in the wok or skillet. Add the sliced beef and stir-fry for about 2–3 minutes, or until seared on all sides.

5 Add the sliced bell pepper and crushed garlic to the pan and continue stir-frying for 2 minutes.

6 Pour the dry sherry and soy sauce into the pan and stir together. Add the sliced scallions. Cook the scallions in the liquid for approximately 1 minute, stirring occasionally. Let the mixture in the pan bubble, but do not let it burn.

7 Transfer the beef stir-fry to warm serving bowls and scatter with the dry-fried sesame seeds. Serve hot with freshly boiled noodles.

COOK'S TIP

You can spread the sesame seeds out on a cookie sheet and toast them under a preheated broiler until browned all over, if you prefer.

Lamb with Mushroom Sauce

Try to use a lean cut of lamb for this simple yet delicious recipe, for both flavor and tenderness.

NUTRITIONAL INFORMATION

Calories	219	Sugars	1g
Protein	21g	Fat	14g
Carbohydrate	4g	Saturates	4g

 5 mins  10 mins

SERVES 4

INGREDIENTS

12 oz/350 g lean, boneless lamb
2 tbsp vegetable oil
3 garlic cloves, crushed
1 leek, sliced
6 oz/175 g large mushrooms, sliced
½ tsp sesame oil
fresh red chiles, to garnish

SAUCE

1 tsp cornstarch
4 tbsp light soy sauce
3 tbsp Chinese rice wine or dry sherry
3 tbsp water
½ tsp chili sauce

1 Using a sharp knife or meat cleaver, cut the lamb into thin strips.

2 Heat the vegetable oil in a preheated wok or large, heavy-bottomed skillet.

3 Add the lamb strips, garlic, and leek, and cook for about 2–3 minutes.

4 To make the sauce, in a bowl mix together the cornstarch, soy sauce, Chinese rice wine or dry sherry, water, and chili sauce and set aside.

5 Add the sliced mushrooms to the pan and cook for 1 minute.

6 Stir in the prepared sauce and cook for 2–3 minutes, or until the lamb is cooked through and tender.

7 Sprinkle the sesame oil over the top and transfer the lamb and mushrooms to a warm serving dish. Garnish with red chiles and serve immediately.

1

5

7

VARIATION

The lamb can be replaced with lean steak or pork tenderloin in this classic recipe from Beijing. You could also use 2–3 scallions, 1 shallot, or 1 small onion, instead of the leek, if you prefer.

Lime Mousse with Mango

Lime-flavored cream molds, served with a fresh mango and lime sauce, make a stunning dessert.

NUTRITIONAL INFORMATION	
Calories 254	Sugars 17g
Protein 5g	Fat 19g
Carbohydrate ...17g	Saturates 12g

10 mins 0 mins

SERVES 4

INGREDIENTS

1 cup plain fromage frais or yogurt

grated zest of 1 lime

1 tbsp superfine sugar

½ cup heavy cream

MANGO SAUCE

1 mango

juice of 1 lime

4 tsp superfine sugar

TO DECORATE

4 ground cherries

strips of lime zest

1 Put the fromage frais, lime zest, and sugar in a bowl and mix together.

2 Whisk the heavy cream in a separate bowl, then fold it into the fromage frais mixture.

3 Line 4 decorative molds or ramekins with cheesecloth or plastic wrap and divide the mixture evenly between them. Fold the cheesecloth or plastic wrap over the top and press down firmly.

4 To make the sauce, slice through the mango on each side of the large, flat pit, then cut the flesh from the pit. Remove the skin and discard.

1

3

5

5 Cut off 12 thin slices and set aside. Chop the remaining mango, put into a food processor with the lime juice and sugar, and blend until smooth. Alternatively, push the mango through a strainer then mix with the lime juice and sugar.

6 Turn out the molds onto serving plates. Arrange 3 mango slices on each plate, pour some sauce around, decorate with ground cherries and lime zest, and serve.

COOK'S TIP

Ground cherries have a tart and mildly scented flavor and make an excellent decoration for many desserts. Peel back the papery husks to expose the bright orange fruits.

Exotic Fruit Salad

This is a sophisticated fruit salad that makes use of some of the exotic fruits that can now be seen in the supermarket.

NUTRITIONAL INFORMATION

Calories	149	Sugars	39g
Protein	1g	Fat	0.1g
Carbohydrate	39g	Saturates	0g

 10 mins  15 mins

SERVES 6

INGREDIENTS

- 3 passion fruit
- ⅔ cup superfine sugar
- ⅔ cup water
- 1 mango
- 10 lychees, canned or fresh
- 1 star fruit

1 Halve the passion fruit and press the flesh through a strainer into a pan.

2 Add the sugar and water to the pan and bring to a gentle boil, stirring.

3 Put the mango on a cutting board and cut a thick slice from either side, cutting as near to the pit as possible. Cut away as much flesh as possible in large chunks from the pit section.

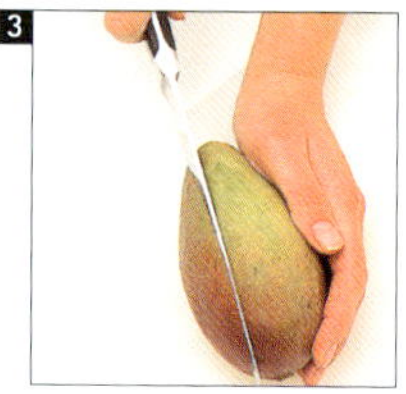
3

4

5

4 Take the 2 side slices and make 3 cuts through the flesh but not the skin, then 3 more cuts at right angles to make a lattice pattern.

5 Push each piece inside out so that the cubed flesh is exposed and you can easily cut it off.

6 Peel and pit the lychees and cut the star fruit into 12 slices.

7 Add all the mango flesh, lychees, and star fruit to the passion fruit syrup and poach gently for 5 minutes. Remove the fruit with a slotted spoon.

8 Bring the syrup to a boil and cook for 5 minutes, until it thickens slightly.

9 To serve, transfer all the fruit to individual serving glasses or bowls, pour over the sugar syrup, and serve warm.

COOK'S TIP

A delicious accompaniment to any exotic fruit dish is cardamom cream. Crush the seeds from 8 cardamom pods, add 1¼ cups whipping cream, and whip until soft peaks form.